Volume 2

CONTENTS

GW00645706

Copyright © 1999 Walton]
3-5 North Frederick Street, Dublin 1, Ireland

Produced by Pat Conway • Photos: The Irish Historical Picture Company
Design by Temple of Design • Printed in Ireland by ColourBooks Ltd.

Order No. wm1320
ISBN No. 1 85720 093 4

Exclusive Distributors:
Walton Manufacturing Co. Ltd., Unit 6A, Rosemount Park Drive, Rosemount Business Park, Ballycoolin Road, Blanchardstown, Dublin 15, Ireland
Walton Music Inc., P.O. Box 874, New York, NY 10009, U.S.A.

1 3 5 7 9 0 8 6 4 2

Grace

Written by Frank & Sean O'Meara about Grace Gifford, who married
Joseph Mary Plunkett on the eve of his execution in Kilmainham Jail in May 1916.

Copyright Asdee Music Ltd.

As we gat - her in the cha - pel here in old Kil - main - ham jail, I think a - bout the last few weeks, oh will they say we've failed? From our school - days they have told us we must yearn for li - ber - ty, Yet all I want in this dark place is to have you here with me.

Chorus

Oh Grace just hold me in your arms, and let this mo - ment lin - ger, Then take me out at dawn, and I will die. With all my love I place this wed - ding ring up - on your fin - ger. There won't be time to share our love, for we must say good - bye.

Now I know it's hard for you, my love, to ever understand
The love I bear for these brave men, my love for this dear land,
But when Padraic called me to his side down in the G.P.O.,
I had to leave my own sick bed, to him I had to go.
Chorus:-

Now as the dawn is breaking, my heart is breaking too,
On this May morn' as I walk out, my thoughts will be of you.
And I'll write some words upon the wall so everyone will know,
I loved so much that I could see his blood upon the rose.
Chorus:-

Blackrock, Co. Dublin

The Gypsy

Traditional
Arrangement Copyright Waltons Publications Ltd.

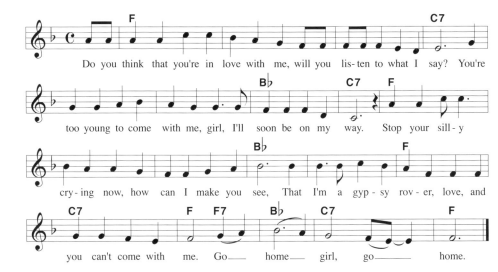

Do you think that you're in love with me, will you lis-ten to what I say? You're
too young to come with me, girl, I'll soon be on my way. Stop your sill-y
cry-ing now, how can I make you see, That I'm a gyp-sy rov-er, love, and
you can't come with me. Go— home— girl, go— home.

You met me at the market when your Ma was not with you,
And you liked my long brown ringlets and my handkerchief of blue.
Although I'm very fond of you and you asked me home to tea,
I am a gypsy rover, love, and you can't come with me.
Go home, girl, go home.

Your brother is a peeler and he would put me in jail,
If he knew I was a poacher and I hunt your lord's best game.
Your Daddy is a gentleman, your Mammy is just as grand,
But I'm a gypsy rover, love, I'll not be your husband.
Go home, girl, go home.

The hour's drawing on, love, and your Ma's expecting thee,
Don't you tell her that you met me here, or I'm a gypsy.
Let's get off my jacket now, your love will have to wait,
For I am twenty-two years old, and you, you're only eight.

Go home, girl, go home.
Go home, girl, go home.

Irish Molly O

A song made famous by the Flanagan Brothers in America during the 1920s.
Words & Music by William Jerome/Jean Schwartz

Mol - ly dear now did you hear the news that's go - ing round?

Down in a cor - ner of my heart, a love is what you've found. And

ev - 'ry time I look in - to your I - rish eyes so blue They

seem to whis - per, 'Dar - ling boy, my love is all for you.' Oh

Chorus

Mol - ly, my I - rish Mol - ly, my sweet a - chus - la dear, I'm fair - ly off my

troll - ey, my I - rish Mol - ly, when you are near. Spring - time you know is ring time.

Come dear now don't be slow. Change your name, go out with game, Be -

gor - ra would - n't I do the same— My I - rish Mol - ly - O.

Molly dear, now did you hear, I furnished up the flat,
Three little cosy rooms with bath and 'welcome' on the mat.
It's five pounds down and two a week, we'll soon be out of debt,
It's all complete except they haven't brought the cradle yet.
Chorus:-

5

No Frontiers

Written by one of Ireland's finest contemporary songwriters, Jimmy MacCarthy.

Copyright Jimmy MacCarthy (MCPS)

Heav - en knows_____ no___ fron - tiers,_____

And I've seen heav - en in___ your__ eyes._____

And if life is a barroom in which we must wait,
Round the man with his fingers on the ivory gate,
Where we sing until dawn of our fears and our fates,
And we stack all the dead men in self addressed crates.
In your eyes, faint as the singing of the lark,
That somehow this black night feels warmer for the spark,
Warmer for the spark,

If your life is a rough bed of brambles and nails,
And your spirit's a slave to man's whips and man's jails
Where you thirst and you hunger for justice and right,
And your heart is a pure flame of man's constant night,
In your eyes, faint as the singing of the lark,
That somehow this black night feels warmer for the spark,
Warmer for the spark,
To hold us till the day when fear will lose its grip,
And heaven has its way, and heaven has its way,
When all will harmonise and know what's in our hearts,
The dream will realise.
Heaven knows no frontiers,
And I've seen heaven in your eyes,
Heaven knows no frontiers,
And I've seen heaven in your eyes.

Red Rose Café

In Holland this Dutch song is known as 'The Little Cafe on the Corner'.
Words & Music by Kartner/Black

Copyright Stemra Music

They come from the for-ests—— and the fac-to-ries—— too, and they all soon for-get who they are. The cares of the day are soon washed a-way, as they sit by a stool in the bar. The girl with green—— eyes in the Roll-ing Stone shirt does-n't look like she walks on the land. The man at—— the end, he's a ve-ry—— good friend of a man who sells cars sec-ond - hand.

Chorus

Down at the Red Rose Ca - fe in the har - bour, There by the port just out - side Am - ster - dam, Eve - ry - one—— shares in the songs and the laugh - ter. Eve - ry - one there is so hap - py—— to be there.——

The salesmen relax with a few pints of beer,
As they try not to speak about trade.
The poet won't write any verses tonight,
He may sing a sweet serenade.
So pull up a chair and forget about life,
It's a good thing to do now and then,
And if you like a deal, I have an idea,
Tomorrow let's all meet again.
Chorus:-

The Cloughmore Tea Gardens, The Quay, Rostrevor, Co. Down

I'll Tell Me Ma

This children's skipping song from Belfast is a great favourite among ballad singers.

Arrangement copyright Waltons Publications Ltd.

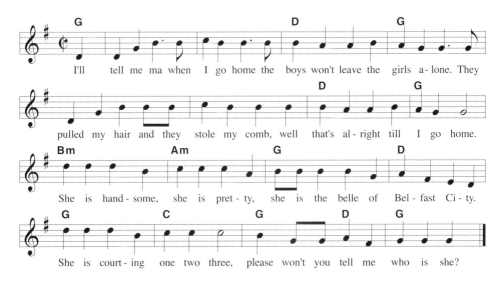

I'll tell me ma when I go home the boys won't leave the girls a-lone. They pulled my hair and they stole my comb, well that's al-right till I go home. She is hand-some, she is pret-ty, she is the belle of Bel-fast Ci-ty. She is court-ing one two three, please won't you tell me who is she?

Albert Mooney says he loves her, all the boys are fighting for her.
They knock at the door and they ring at the bell, saying, 'Oh my true-love, are you well?'
Out she comes, as white as snow, rings on her fingers and bells on her toes.
Old Johnny Murray says she'll die, if she doesn't get the fellow with the roving eye.

Let the wind and the rain and the hail blow high, and the snow come tumbling from the sky,
She's as nice as apple pie, she'll get her own lad by and by.
When she gets a lad of her own, she won't tell her ma when she goes home,
Let them all come as they will, for it's Albert Mooney she loves still.

Cable Road, Whitehead, Co. Antrim

10

The Star of the County Down

The words to this song were written by Cathal MacGarvey, who died in 1927. The air is 'My Love Nell'.

Arrangement copyright Waltons Publications Ltd.

Near— Ban-bridge town in the Coun-ty Down one— mor-ning in Ju - ly, Down a bo-reen green came a sweet col - leen and she smiled as she passed me by. She looked so sweet from her two bare feet to the sheen of her nut-brown— hair. Such a coax-ing elf that I shook my-self to make sure she was rea-lly there. From Ban-try Bay up to Der-ry Quay and from Gal-way to Dub-lin— town, No— maid I've seen like the sweet col-leen that I met in the Coun-ty Down.

As she onward sped, sure I shook my head, and I looked with a feeling rare,
And I said, says I, to a passer-by, 'Who's the maid with the nut-brown hair?'
He smiled at me and with pride says he, 'That's the gem of Ireland's crown,
Young Rosie McCann from the Banks of the Bann, she's the star of the County Down.'
Chorus:-

At the harvest fair she'll be surely there, so I'll dress in my Sunday clothes,
With my shoes shone bright and my hat cocked right, for a smile from my nut-brown rose.
No pipe I'll smoke, no horse I'll yoke, though my plough with rust turn brown,
Till a smiling bride by my own fireside sits the star of the County Down.
Chorus:-

The Hills of Kerry

Traditional

Arrangement copyright Waltons Publications Ltd.

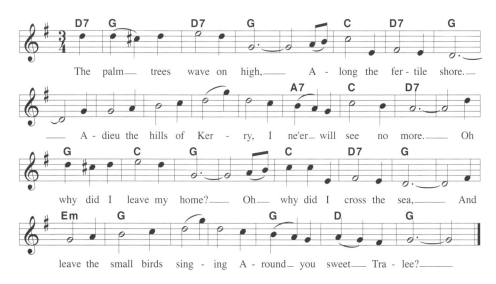

The palm— trees wave on high,— A - long the fer - tile shore.—
— A - dieu the hills of Ker - ry, I ne'er— will see no more.— Oh
why did I leave my home?— Oh— why did I cross the sea,— And
leave the small birds sing - ing A - round— you sweet— Tra - lee?—

Middle Lake, Killarney, Co. Kerry

The noble and the brave
Have departed from our shore.
They've gone off to a foreign land,
Where the wild cannons roar.
No more they'll see the shamrock,
The plant so dear to me,
Or hear the small birds singing
Around sweet Tralee.
Repeat first verse:—

No more the sun will shine
On that blessed harvest morn,
Or hear our reaper singing
In a golden field of corn.
There's a balm for every woe,
And a cure for every pain,
But the happiness of my darling girl
I never will see again.
Repeat first verse:—

An Irish Peasant Girl

The Lowlands Low

Traditional

Arrangement copyright Waltons Publications Ltd.

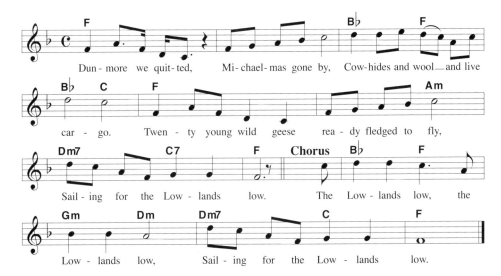

Dun - more we quit - ted, Mi - chael - mas gone by, Cow-hides and wool — and live car - go. Twen - ty young wild geese rea - dy fledged to fly, Sail - ing for the Low - lands low. The Low - lands low, the Low - lands low, Sail - ing for the Low - lands low.

Shaun Paor's the skipper, from the church of Crook,
Piery keeps log for his father.
Crew all from Bannow, Fethard and the Hook,
Sailing for the Lowlands Low.
Chorus:- (repeat after each verse)

These twenty Wild Geese gave Queen Anne the slip,
Crossing to Louis in Flanders.
He and Jack Malbrook both are in a grip,
Fighting in the Lowlands Low.

Close lay a rover off the Isle of Wight,
Either a Salee or Saxon.
Out through a sea mist we bade them good night,
Sailing for the Lowlands Low.

Ready with priming we'd our galliot gun,
Muskets and pikes in good order.
We should be riddled, captives would be none.
Death! or else the Lowlands Low.

Pray, holy Brendan, Turk or Algerine,
Dutchman nor Saxon may sink us.
We'll bring back Geneva Rack and Rhenish wine,
Safely from the Lowlands Low.

14

Mary from Dungloe

The annual 'Mary from Dungloe Festival' is held every July in Dungloe, Co. Donegal.
Arrangement copyright Waltons Publications Ltd.

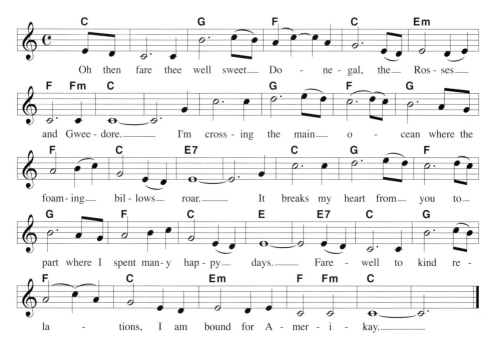

Oh then fare thee well sweet Donegal, the Roses and Gwee-dore. I'm crossing the main ocean where the foam-ing bil-lows roar. It breaks my heart from you to part where I spent man-y hap-py days. Fare-well to kind re-la-tions, I am bound for A-mer-i-kay.

Oh my love is tall and handsome, and her age is scarce eighteen,
She far exceeds all other fair maids, when she trips o'er the green.
Her lovely neck and shoulders are fairer than the snow,
Till the day I die I'll ne'er deny my Mary from Dungloe.

If I was home in sweet Dungloe a letter I would write,
Kind thoughts would fill my bosom, for Mary my delight.
'Tis in her father's garden the fairest violets grow,
And 'twas there I came to court the maid, my Mary from Dungloe.

Oh then Mary you're my heart's delight, my pride and only care,
It was your cruel father would not let me stay there.
But absence makes the heart grow fond, and when I am over the main,
May the Lord protect my darling girl until I return again.

And I wish I was in sweet Dungloe, and seated on the grass,
And by my side a bottle of wine, and on my knee a lass.
I'd call for liquor of the best, and I'd pay before I'd go,
And I'd roll my Mary in my arms, in the town of sweet Dungloe.

Avondale

Avondale House, Co. Wicklow, was the home of Charles Stuart Parnell (1846-1891),
President of the Land League and leader of the Home Rule Party.

Arrangement copyright Waltons Publications Ltd.

Oh have you been to A - von - dale, and ling - ered in its love - ly vale, Where tall trees whis - per and know the tale of Av - on - dale's proud ea - gle?

Where pride and ancient glory fade, so was the land where he was laid.
Like Christ was thirty pieces paid for Avondale's proud eagle.
Repeat first verse:—

Long years that green and lovely vale has nursed Parnell, her grandest Gael.
And curse the land that has betrayed fair Avondale's proud eagle.
Repeat first verse:—

Avondale, Co. Wicklow

The Old Woman from Wexford

This popular ballad is found in the Sam Henry *Collection* and many others.
Arrangement copyright Waltons Publications Ltd.

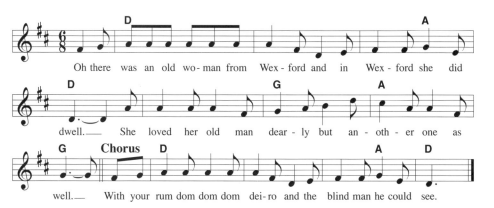

Oh there was an old wo- man from Wex - ford and in Wex - ford she did dwell.— She loved her old man dear - ly but an - oth - er one as well.— With your rum dom dom dom dei- ro and the blind man he could see.

One day she went to the doctor, some medicine for to find.
She said, 'Will you give me something for to make me old man blind?'
Chorus:- (repeat after each verse)

'Feed him eggs and marrowbones and make him suck them all,
And it won't be very long after till he won't see you at all.'

The doctor wrote a letter and he signed it with his hand,
He sent it round to the old man just to let him understand.

She fed him eggs and marrowbones and made him suck them all,
And it wasn't very long after till he couldn't see the wall.

Says he, 'I'd like to drown myself, but that might be a sin.'
Says she, 'I'll go along with you and help to push you in.'

The woman she stepped back a bit to rush and push him in,
And the old man quickly stepped aside and she went tumblin' in.

Oh, how loudly she did roar and how loudly she did call.
'Yerra, hold your whist old woman, sure I can't see you at all.'

Now eggs, or eggs and marrowbones, may make your old man blind,
But if you want to drown him, you must creep up close behind.

Dan O'Hara

Traditional

Arrangement copyright Waltons Publications Ltd.

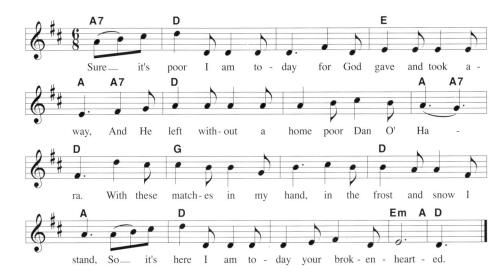

Sure— it's poor I am to-day for God gave and took a-way, And He left with-out a home poor Dan O' Ha-ra. With these match-es in my hand, in the frost and snow I stand, So— it's here I am to-day your brok-en-heart-ed.

In the year of sixty-four, I had acres by the score
And the grandest land you ever ran a plough through.
But the landlord came you know, and he laid our old home low,
So it's here I am today your broken-hearted.
Repeat first verse:—

For twenty years or more did misfortune cross our door,
And my poor old wife and I were sadly parted.
We were scattered far and wide and our children starved and died,
So it's here I am today your broken-hearted.
Repeat first verse:—

Tho' in frost and snow I stand, sure the shadow of God's hand,
It lies warm about the brow of Dan O'Hara.
And soon with God above I will meet the ones I love,
And I'll find the joys I lost in Connemara.
Repeat first verse:—

The Wearing of the Green

Dion Lardner Boursiquot (Dion Boucicault) was born in Dublin on Boxing Day, 1820 or 1822. He lived in London, became a successful playwright and moved to New York where he taught acting. He died in 1890.

Arrangement copyright Waltons Publications Ltd.

Oh— Pad-dy dear, and did you hear the news that's go-ing round? The Sham-rock is for-bid by law to grow on Ir-ish ground. No— more St. Pat-rick's Day we'll keep, his col-ours can't be seen, For there's a cru-el law a-gainst the wear-ing of the green. I— met with Nap-per Tan-dy and he took me by the hand, And he said, 'How's poor old Ire-land and how— does she stand?' 'She's the most dis-tress-ful count-ry that e-ver yet was seen, For they're hang-ing men and wo-men for the wear-ing of the green.'

And if the colour we must wear is England's cruel Red,
Let it remind us of the blood that Ireland has shed.
Then pull the shamrock from your hat, and throw it on the sod,
And never fear, 'twill take root there, tho' under foot 'tis trod.

When the law can stop the blades of grass from growing as they grow,
And when the leaves in summer-time, their colour dare not show,
Then I will change the colour, too, I wear in my caubeen,
But till that day, please God, I'll stick to wearing of the Green.

Bright Blue Rose

Words & Music by Jimmy MacCarthy

Copyright Jimmy MacCarthy (MCPS)

I skimmed a-cross Black-wa-ter with-out once sub-merg-ing on-to the banks of an ur-ban morn-ing,— That hun-gers— the first light much, much more than the moun-tains e - ver do, And she, like a ghost be-side me, goes down with the ease of a dol-phin, And— e-mer-ges un - learned, un-shamed, un-harmed, For she— is the per-fect crea-ture, na-tu-ral in eve-ry fea-ture, And I— am the geek— with the al-chem-ist's stone. For all of you who must dis-co-ver, For all who seek to un-der-stand, For hav-ing left the path of o - thers, You'll find a ve-ry spe-cial hand. And

it is a ho-ly thing, and it is a pre-cious time, And it is the on - ly way. For - get - me - nots a- mong the snow, It's al-ways been and so it goes, To pon - der his death, and his life e - ter - na - lly.

And it is a holy thing,
And it is a precious time,
And it is the only way.
Forget-me-nots among the snow,
It's always been and so it goes,
To ponder his life and his death eternally.

One bright blue rose,
Outlives all those,
Two thousand years and still it goes,
To ponder his life and his death eternally.

She Moved Through the Fair

Padraig Colum, the famous Irish poet, set new words to this air, originally collected by Herbert Hughes in Co. Donegal.

Copyright Boosey & Hawkes Music Publishers Ltd.

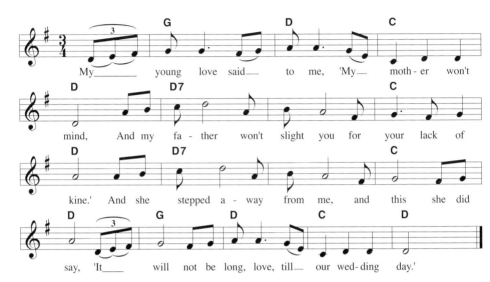

She went away from me, and went through the fair,
And fondly I watched her move here and move there.
Then she went her way homeward with one star awake,
As the swan, in the evening, moves over the lake.

The people were saying no two were e'er wed,
But one has a sorrow that never was said.
And I smiled as she passed with her goods and her gear,
And that was the last that I saw of my dear.

Last night she came to me, my young love she came in,
So softly she came that her feet made no din.
She laid her hand on me and this she did say,
'It will not be long, love, till our wedding day.'

The Whistling Gypsy

Words & Music by Leo Maguire

Copyright Waltons Publications Ltd.

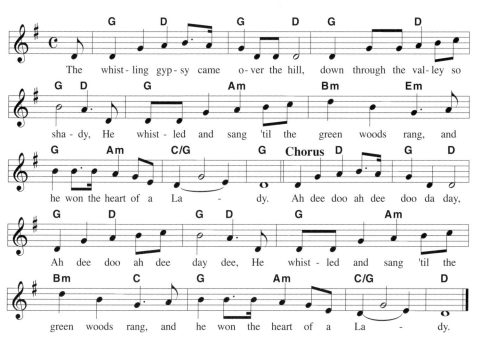

The whist-ling gyp-sy came o-ver the hill, down through the val-ley so sha-dy, He whist-led and sang 'til the green woods rang, and he won the heart of a La - dy. Ah dee doo ah dee doo da day, Ah dee doo ah dee day dee, He whist-led and sang 'til the green woods rang, and he won the heart of a La - dy.

She left her father's castle gate, she left her fair young lover,
She left her servants and estate to follow the gypsy rover.
Chorus:-

Her father saddled up his fastest steed, he ranged the valley over.
He sought his daughter at great speed, and the whistling gypsy rover.
Chorus:-

He came at last to a mansion fine, down by the river Clady,
And there was music and there was wine for the gypsy and his lady.
Chorus:-

'He's no gypsy, father dear, but lord of these lands all over,
I'm going to stay till my dying day with my whistling gypsy rover.'
Chorus:-

From Clare to Here

Words & Music by Ralph McTell

Copyright Misty River Music Ltd.

When Friday night comes around Eddie's only into fighting,
Me ma would like a letter home but I'm too tired for writing.
Chorus:-

And the only time I feel alright is when I'm into drinking,
It eases off the pain a bit and levels out my thinking.
Chorus:-

Well it almost breaks my heart when I think of Josephine,
I promised I'd be coming back with pockets full of green.
Chorus:-

I dream I hear a piper play, maybe it's emotion,
I dream I see white horses dance upon that other ocean.
Chorus:-

Church Street, Ennis, Co. Clare

The Little Beggarman

Traditional

Arrangement copyright Waltons Publications Ltd.

I am a litt-le beg-gar-man, a-beg-ging I have been. For fif-ty years or more— in this lit-tle isle of green, And— up to the Lif-fey and down to Tes-sa-gue, and I'm known — by the name — of the bold John-ny Dhu.

Chorus

Of all the trades of liv-ing sure— beg-ging is the best, For— when a man is tired— he can sit — down and rest. He can beg for a liv-ing, he's got no-thing else to do. But — run a-round the cor-ner with his old ric-a-doo.

I slept last night in a barn at Currabawn.
A wet night came on and I slipped through the door,
Holes in me shoes and the toes peepin' through,
Singin' skiddy-me-re-me-doodlum for ould Johnny Dhu.
Chorus:-

I must be gettin' home, for it's gettin' late at night,
The fire's all raked and there isn't any light.
And now you've heard me story of the old ricadoo.
It's good-night and God bless you from ould Johnnie Dhu.
Chorus:-

The Jug of Punch

A jug was and still is the best for drinking punch from.
As they say, the water and spirits mix better.

Arrangement copyright Waltons Publications Ltd.

What more diversion can a man desire, than to be seated by a snug coal fire,
Upon his knee a pretty wench and on the table a jug of punch.
Chorus:-

If I were sick and very bad, and was not able to go or stand,
I would not think it at all amiss to pledge my shoes for a jug of punch.
Chorus:-

The doctor fails with all his art to cure an impression on the heart,
But if life was gone, within an inch, what would bring it back but a jug of punch?
Chorus:-

But when I'm dead and in my grave, no costly tombstone will I have.
Lay me down in my native peat, with a jug of punch at my head and feet.
Chorus:-

Carrying Wood

The Curragh of Kildare

This song is included in the Joyce *Collection*. The music and lyrics were
written around 1852, taken from Kate Ludmore of Co. Limerick.
Arrangement copyright Waltons Publications Ltd.

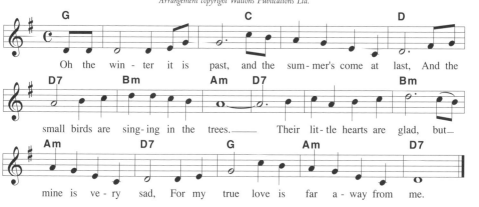

Oh the win - ter it is past, and the sum - mer's come at last, And the small birds are sing- ing in the trees.___ Their lit- tle hearts are glad, but__ mine is ve - ry sad, For my true love is far a - way from me.

All you that are in love, and cannot it remove,
I pity all the pain that you endure.
For experience let me know that your heart is full of woe,
It's a woe that no mortal can endure.

A livery I'll wear, and I'll comb back my hair,
And in velvet so green I will appear,
And straight I will repair to the Curragh of Kildare,
For it's there I'll find tidings of my dear.

Market Square, Kildare

29

The Mermaid

Traditional

Arrangement copyright Waltons Publications Ltd.

It was Fri-day— morn when we— set— sail, and we were not far from the land,_____ When our Cap-tain he spied a mer - maid so fair with a comb and a glass in her hand._____ **Chorus** And the o - cean waves do roll,_____ And the storm - y winds do blow,_____ And we poor— sail-ors are skip-ping at the top, While the land-lub-bers lie down be-low be-low be - low, While the land - lub-bers lie down be - low._____

Then up spoke the captain of our gallant ship, and a fine old sea-dog was he,
'This fishy mermaid has warned me of our doom, we shall sink to the bottom of the sea.'
Chorus:- (repeat after each verse)

Then up spoke the mate of our gallant ship, and a fine-spoken man was he,
Saying, 'I have a wife in Brooklyn by the sea, and tonight a widow she will be.'

Then up spoke the cabin boy of our gallant ship, and a brave young lad was he,
'Oh I have a sweetheart in Salem by the sea, and tonight she'll be weeping for me.'

Then up spoke the cook of our gallant ship, and a crazy old butcher was he,
'I care much more for my pots and my pans, than I do for the bottom of the sea.'

Then three times 'round spun our gallant ship, and three times 'round spun she,
Three times round spun our gallant ship, and she sank to the bottom of the sea.

The Holy Ground

This song, set in Cobh, Co. Cork, is still popular in that part of the county.
The actual site known as the 'Holy Ground' is situated on the east side of the town.

Arrangement copyright Waltons Publications Ltd.

And now the storm is coming, I see it rising soon,
For the night is dark and dreary, you can scarcely see the moon.
And the good old ship she is tossing about, and the rigging is all tore,
But still I live in hope to see the Holy Ground once more.
Chorus:-

And now the storm is over, and we are safe on shore,
And we'll go into a public house to the girls we do adore.
And we'll drink strong ale and porter, and we'll make the rafters roar,
And when our money is all spent, we'll go to sea once more.
Chorus:-

31

The Village Pump

Carrickfergus

This evocative song is set in Carrickfergus, Co. Antrim. The words are a translation from the Irish.

Arrangement copyright Waltons Publications Ltd.

I wish I was in Car-rick Fer - gus on-ly for nights in Bal-ly-gran. I would swim ov-er the deep-est o - cean, the deep-est o - cean for my love to find. But the sea is wide and I can-not swim o - ver and nei-ther have I wings to fly. If I could find me a hand-some boat - man, to fer-ry me o - ver to my love and die.

My childhood days bring back sad reflections, of happy times I spent so long ago.
My boyhood friends and my own relations, have all passed on now like melting snow.
But I'll spend my days in endless roaming, soft is the grass I walk, my bed is free.
Ah! to be back now in Carrickfergus, on that long road down to the sea.

Now in Kilkenny, it is reported, there are marble stones as black as ink.
With gold and silver I would support her, but I'll sing no more now till I get a drink.
I'm drunk today, and I'm seldom sober, a handsome rover from town to town.
Ah! but I'm sick now, my days are numbered, come all ye young men and lay me down.

The Wild Rover

This is a popular ballad in several countries, including Ireland. It tells the story of
the roving carefree man, fond of his drink and a good time.

Arrangement copyright Waltons Publications Ltd.

I've been a wild ro-ver for ma-ny the year,— and I spent all my
mon-ey on whis-key and beer.— But now I'm re-turn-ing with
gold in great store,— And I ne-ver will play the wild ro-ver no
more. And it's no nay ne-ver,— no nay ne-ver no more—
— Will I play— the wild ro-ver,— nay ne-ver— no more.—

I went to an ale-house I used to frequent,
And I told the landlady my money was spent.
I asked her for credit, she answered me, 'Nay,
Such a custom like yours I could have any day.'
Chorus:-

I took from my pocket ten sovereigns bright,
And the landlady's eyes opened wide with delight.
She said, 'I have whiskey and wines of the best,
And the words that I spoke sure were only in jest.'
Chorus:-

I'll go home to my parents, confess what I've done,
And I'll ask them to pardon their prodigal son.
And if they caress me as oft times before,
Sure I never will play the wild rover no more.
Chorus:-

Dicey Riley

This Dublin street ballad concerns a lady who is very fond of the sup (drink).

Arrangement copyright Waltons Publications Ltd.

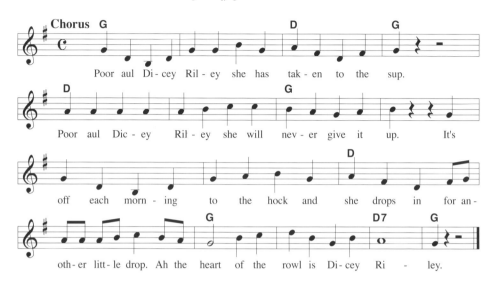

Poor aul Di-cey Ril-ey she has tak-en to the sup.
Poor aul Dic-ey Ril-ey she will nev-er give it up. It's
off each morn-ing to the hock and she drops in for an-
oth-er litt-le drop. Ah the heart of the rowl is Di-cey Ri - ley.

Nelson's Pillar, Dublin

She walks along Fitzgibbon Street
With an independent air.
And then it's down by Summerhill,
And the people stop and stare.
She says it's nearly half past one,
It's time I had another little one.
Ah the heart of the rowl is Dicey Riley.
Chorus:-

She owns a little sweetshop
At the corner of the street.
Every evening, after school,
I go to wash her feet.
She leaves me there to mind the shop,
While she nips out for another little drop.
Ah the heart of the rowl is Dicey Riley.
Chorus:-

My Singing Bird

A beautiful song written by Edith Wheeler.

Arrangement copyright Waltons Publications Ltd.

I've— seen the lark soar— high at morn, to— sing— up— in the blue. I've

heard the black-bird— pipe his song, the— thrush— and the lin-net too.

But— none of them can sing so sweet, my sing-ing bird— as— you.

Ah— my— sing - ing— bird as you.

If I could lure my singing bird from its own cosy nest,
If I could catch my singing bird, I'd warm it on my breast.
And on my heart my singing bird would sing itself to rest,
Ah- would sing itself to rest.

Striking a Bargain

Peggy Gordon

This song, of Scottish origin, concerns the trials and tribulations of love.

Arrangement copyright Waltons Publications Ltd.

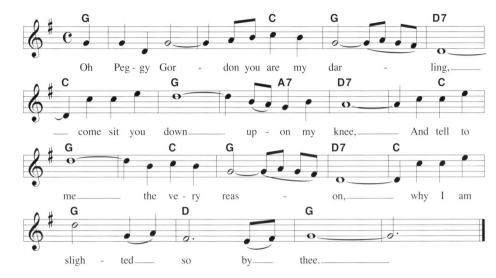

Oh Peg-gy Gor - don you are my dar - ling,___ come sit you down___ up - on my knee,___ And tell to me___ the ve - ry reas - on,___ why I am sligh - ted___ so by___ thee.___

I'm so in love that I can't deny it, my heart lies smothered in my breast,
But it's not for you to let the world know it, a troubled mind can know no rest.

I put my head to a glass of brandy, it was my fancy, I do declare,
For when I'm drinking, I'm always thinking, and wishing Peggy Gordon was here.

I wish I was in some lonesome valley, where womankind cannot be found,
Where the little birds sing upon the branches, and every moment a different sound.

I wish I was away in England, far across the briny sea,
Or sailing o'er the deepest ocean, where care and trouble can't bother me.

Oh Peggy Gordon, you are my darling, come sit you down upon my knee,
And tell to me the very reason, why I am slighted so by thee.

Kelly of Killane

Written by P.J. McCall, this song deals with events during the 1798 Rebellion.
John Kelly, the son of a Killane merchant, was hanged after the battle of New Ross.

Arrangement copyright Waltons Publications Ltd.

What's the news, what's the news O my bold Shel- ma - lier With your long- barr- elled gun— from the sea?—— Say what wind from the south blows his mes - sen- ger here With a hymn of the dawn— for the free?—— Good- ly news, good- ly news, do I bring Youth of Forth, Good- ly news shall you hear Bar - gy man.——— For the boys march at morn from the South to the North, Led by Kel- ly, the Boy— from Kill - ane.———

Tell me who is that giant with the gold curling hair,
He who rides at the head of your band?
Seven feet is his height with some inches to spare
And he looks like a king in command!
Ah, my lads, that's the pride of the bold Shelmaliers,
Among our greatest of heroes a man!
Fling your beavers aloft and give three ringing cheers
For John Kelly, the Boy from Killane.

Market Square, Clifden, Co. Galway 40

The Hills of Connemara

This is a song about the production of illicit alcohol (poteen) and
the attempt by the excise officers to control it.

Arrangement copyright Waltons Publications Ltd.

Gath-er up the pots and the old tin can, the mash, the corn, the bar-ley and the bran.

Run like the dev-il from the ex-cise man, keep the smoke from ris-ing Bar-ney.

Keep your eyes well peeled today, the tall, tall men are on their way,
Searching for the mountain tay, in the hills of Connemara.

Swing to the left and swing to the right, the excise men will dance all night,
Drinking up the tay till the broad daylight, in the hills of Connemara.

A gallon for the butcher, a quart for Tom, a bottle for poor old Father Tom,
To help the poor old dear along, in the hills of Connemara.

Stand your ground, it is too late, the excise men are at the gate,
Glory be to Paddy but they're drinking it nate, in the hills of Connemara.

Excise Officers Seizing Whiskey at Innishowen

The Meeting of the Waters

Written by Thomas Moore (1779-1852). The 'Meeting of the Waters' is the meeting
of the Avonmore and Avonbeg rivers in Avoca, Co. Wicklow.
Arrangement copyright Waltons Publications Ltd.

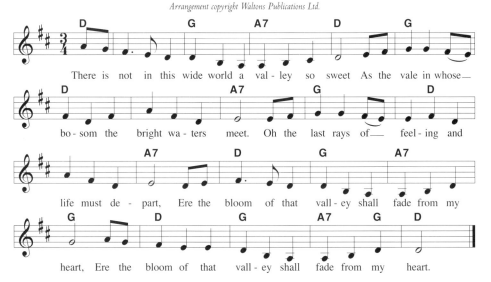

There is not in this wide world a val - ley so sweet As the vale in whose —
bo - som the bright wa - ters meet. Oh the last rays of — feel - ing and
life must de - part, Ere the bloom of that vall - ey shall fade from my
heart, Ere the bloom of that vall - ey shall fade from my heart.

Yet it was not that nature had shed o'er the scene
Her purest of crystal and brightest of green.
'Twas not her soft magic of streamlet or hill,
Oh no, it was something more exquisite still.

'Twas that friends, the beloved of my bosom, were near,
Who made every dear scene of enchantment more dear,
And who felt how the best charms of Nature improve
When we see them reflected from looks that we love.

Sweet Vale of Avoca! how calm could I rest
In thy bosom of shade, with the friends I love best,
Where the storms that we feel in this cold world should cease,
And our hearts, like thy waters, be mingled in peace.

James Connolly

James Connolly, patriot, trade unionist and Commander of the Republican Army in 1916, was wounded and taken prisoner. Unable to stand due to his wounds, he was executed sitting in a chair on 12th May 1916.

Arrangement copyright Waltons Publications Ltd.

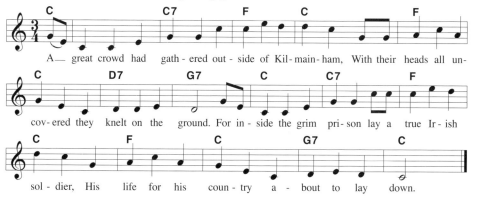

A— great crowd had gath - ered out - side of Kil - main - ham, With their heads all un-cov - ered they knelt on the ground. For in - side the grim pri - son lay a true Ir - ish sol - dier, His life for his coun - try a - bout to lay down.

He went to his death like a true son of Ireland,
The firing party he bravely did face.
Then the order rang out: 'Present arms, Fire!'
James Connolly fell into a ready-made grave.

The black flag they hoisted, the cruel deed was over,
Gone was the man who loved Ireland so well.
There was many a sad heart in Dublin that morning,
When they murdered James Connolly, the Irish rebel.

Many years have rolled by since the Irish Rebellion
When the guns of Britannia they loudly did speak.
And the bold I.R.A. they stood shoulder to shoulder,
And the blood from their bodies flowed down Sackville Street.

The Four Courts of Dublin the English bombarded,
The spirit of freedom they tried hard to quell.
But above all the din came the cry: 'No Surrender!'
'Twas the voice of James Connolly, the Irish rebel.

Connemara Cradle Song

Originally written by John Frances Waller (1809-1894),
this song was popularised by Mayo-born Delia Murphy (1902-1971).

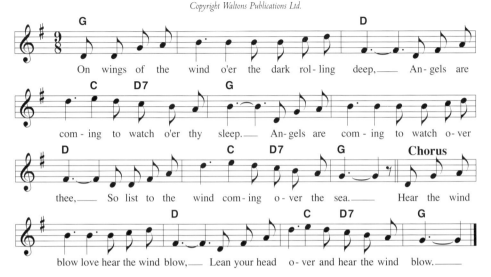

On wings of the wind o'er the dark rol-ling deep,⸺ An-gels are
com-ing to watch o'er thy sleep.⸺ An-gels are com-ing to watch o-ver
thee,⸺ So list to the wind com-ing o-ver the sea.⸺ Hear the wind
blow love hear the wind blow,⸺ Lean your head o-ver and hear the wind blow.⸺

Oh, winds of the night, may your fury be crossed,
May no one who's dear to our island be lost.
Blow the wind lightly, calm be the foam,
Shine the light brightly to guide them all home.
Chorus:-

The currachs are sailing way out on the blue,
Chasing the herring of silvery hue.
Silver the herring and silver the sea,
Soon there'll be silver for baby and me.
Chorus:-

The currachs, tomorrow, will stand on the shore,
And daddy'll go sailing, a-sailing no more.
The nets will be drying, the nets heaven blessed,
And safe in my arms dear, contented he'll rest.
Chorus:-

The Cliffs of Dooneen

Dooneen Point lies six miles north of Ballybunion, Co. Kerry.

Arrangement copyright Waltons Publications Ltd.

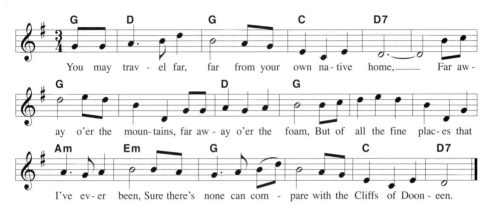

You may trav - el far, far from your own na - tive home,___ Far aw -
ay o'er the moun - tains, far aw - ay o'er the foam, But of all the fine plac - es that
I've ev - er been, Sure there's none can com - pare with the Cliffs of Doon - een.

Take a view o'er the mountains, fine sights you'll see there,
You'll see the high rocky mountains o'er the west coast of Clare.
Oh, the towns of Kilkee and Kilrush can be seen,
From the high rocky slopes 'round the Cliffs of Dooneen.

It's a nice place to be on a fine summer's day,
Watching all the wild flowers that ne'er do decay.
Oh, the hares and lofty pheasants are plain to be seen,
Making homes for their young 'round the Cliffs of Dooneen.

Fare thee well to Dooneen, fare thee well for a while,
And to all the kind people I'm leaving behind,
To the streams and the meadows where late I have been,
And the high rocky slopes 'round the Cliffs of Dooneen.

Johnny I Hardly Knew Ye

The lyrics of this famous anti-war song are thought to date from the 19th c., when the British
government recruited Irishmen to fight in India. Patrick Gilmore is credited with writing the song.

Arrangement copyright Waltons Publications Ltd.

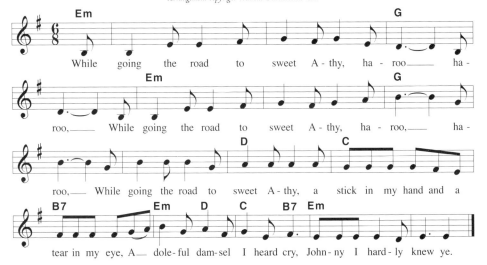

Chorus: (repeat after each verse)
With your drums and guns and guns and drums, ha-roo, haroo,
With your drums and guns and guns and drums, ha-roo, ha-roo,
With your drums and guns and guns and drums, the enemy nearly slew ye.
My darling dear, you look so queer, och, Johnny, I hardly knew ye!

Where are your eyes that looked so mild, ha-roo, ha-roo,
Where are your eyes that looked so mild, ha-roo, ha-roo,
Where are your eyes that looked so mild, when my poor heart you first beguiled?
Why did you run from me and the child, Johnny, I hardly knew ye!

Where are the legs with which you run, ha-roo, ha-roo,
Where are the legs with which you run, ha-roo, ha-roo,
Where are the legs with which you run, when you went to carry a gun?
Indeed your dancing days are done, Johnny, I hardly knew ye!

It grieved my heart to see you sail, ha-roo, ha-roo,
It grieved my heart to see you sail, ha-roo, ha-roo,
It grieved my heart to see you sail, though from my heart you took leg bail.
Like a cod you're doubled up head and tail, Johnny, I hardly knew ye!

You haven't an arm and you haven't a leg, ha-roo, ha-roo,
You haven't an arm and you haven't a leg, ha-roo, ha-roo,
You haven't an arm and you haven't a leg, you're an eyeless, noseless, chickenless egg.
You'll have to be put in a bowl to beg, Johnny, I hardly knew ye!

I'm happy for to see you home, ha-roo, ha-roo,
I'm happy for to see you home, ha-roo, ha-roo,
I'm happy for to see you home, all from the Island of Sulloon,
So low in flesh, so high in bone, Johnny, I hardly knew ye!

But sad as it is to see you so, ha-roo, ha-roo,
But sad as it is to see you so, ha-roo, ha-roo,
But sad as it is to see you so, and I think of you now as an object of woe,
Your Peggy'll still keep ye on as her beau, Johnny, I hardly knew ye!

Leinster House, Dublin

47

Do You Want Your Old Lobby Washed Down?

This song originates from Co. Cork. It is said that washing down the lobby or
hallway of the house was accepted by the landlord as part payment of rent.

Arrangement copyright Waltons Publications Ltd.

I've a nice lit-tle cot and a small bit of land And a place by the side of the sea.___ And I care a-bout no one be-cause I be-lieve That no-bo-dy cares a-bout me.___ My peace is de-stroyed and I'm fair-ly a-nnoyed By a lass-ie who works in the town.___ She sighs ev-'ry day as she pass-es the way, 'Do you want your old lob-by washed down?___ Do you want your old lob-by washed down Con Shine? Do you want your old lob-by washed down?'___ She sighs ev-'ry day as she pass-es the way, 'Do you want your old lob-by washed down?'___

Chorus

The other day the old landlord came by for his rent,
I told him no money I had.
Besides 'twasn't fair for to ask me to pay,
The times were so awfully bad.
He felt discontent at not getting his rent,
And he shook his big head in a frown.
Says he, 'I'll take half,' but says I with a laugh,
'Do you want your old lobby washed down?'
Chorus:-

Now the boys look so bashful when they go out courting,
They seem to look so very shy,
As to kiss a young maid, sure they seem half afraid,
But they would if they could on the sly.
But me, I do things in a different way,
I don't give a nod or a frown.
When I goes to court I says, 'Here goes for sport.
Do you want your old lobby washed down?'
Chorus:-

Wool Washing, Irish Coast

49

The Boston Burglar

Traditional

Arrangement copyright Waltons Publications Ltd.

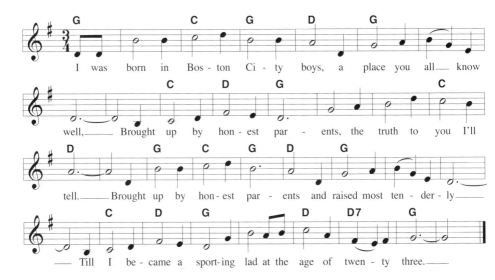

I was born in Bos - ton Ci - ty, boys, a place you all__ know well,__ Brought up by hon - est par - ents, the truth to you I'll tell.__ Brought up by hon - est par - ents and raised most ten - der - ly__ __ Till I be - came a sport-ing lad at the age of twen - ty three.__

My character was taken and I was sent to jail,
My parents tried to bail me out, but found it all in vain.
The jury found me guilty, the clerk he wrote it down,
The judge he passed my sentence, I was sent to Charlestown.

I see my aged father, and he standing by the Bar,
Likewise my aged mother, and she tearing of her hair,
The tearing of her old grey locks, and the tears came mingled down,
Saying, 'Johnny, my son, what have you done, that you're bound for Charlestown?'

There's a girl in Boston City, boys, a place you all know well,
And if e'er I get my liberty, it's with her I will dwell.
If e'er I get my liberty, bad company I will shun,
The robbing of the Munster Bank, and the drinking of rum.

You lads that are at liberty, should keep it while you can,
Don't roam the street by night or day, or break the laws of man.
For if you do you're sure to rue and become a lad like me,
A-serving up your twenty-one years, in the Royal Artillery.

The Croppy Boy

The rebels of the Rising of 1798 were called 'Croppies' on account of their short cropped hair, cut in the style of the French Revolutionaries. Written by William McBurney under the pseudonym Carroll Malone.
Arrangement copyright Waltons Publications Ltd.

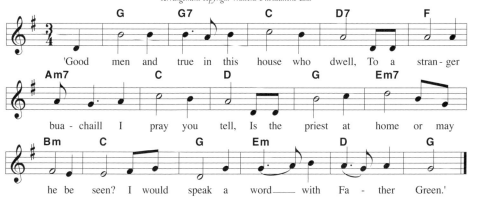

'The priest's at home, boy, and may be seen, 'tis easy speaking with Father Green,
But you must wait till I go and see if the holy father alone may be.'

The youth has entered an empty hall, what a lonely sound has his light footfall,
And the gloomy chamber's cold and bare, with a vested priest in a lonely chair.

The youth has knelt to tell his sins, 'Nomine Dei' the youth begins.
At 'mea culpa' he beats his breast, then in broken murmurs he speaks the rest.

'At the siege of Ross did my father fall, and at Gorey my loving brothers all.
I alone am left of my name and race, I will go to Wexford to take their place.'

'I cursed three times since last Easter day, and at Mass-time once I went to play.
I passed the churchyard one day in haste, and forgot to pray for my mother's rest.'

'I bear no hate against living thing, but I love my country above my king.
Now Father, bless me and let me go, to die if God has ordained it so.'

The priest said naught, but a rustling noise made the youth look up in a wild surprise.
The robes were off, and in scarlet there, sat a yeoman captain with fiery glare.

With fiery glare and with fury hoarse, instead of a blessing he breathed a curse.
'Twas a good thought, boy, to come here and shrive, for one short hour is your time to live.

Upon yon river three tenders float, the priest's on one, if he isn't shot.
We hold this house for our lord and king, and Amen say I, may all traitors swing!'

At Geneva Barracks that young man died, and at Passage they have his body laid.
Good people who live in peace and joy, breathe a prayer, shed a tear, for the Croppy Boy.

The Castle of Dromore

The Castle of Dromore is situated on the river Blackwater, on the ring of Kerry.

Arrangement copyright Waltons Publications Ltd.

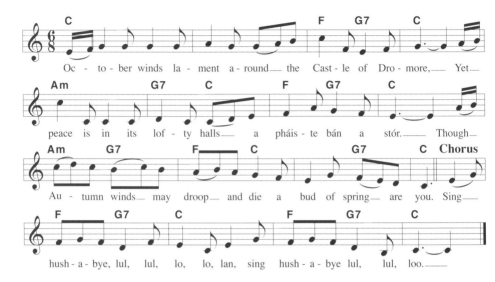

Oc - to - ber winds la - ment a - round— the Cast - le of Dro - more,— Yet—
peace is in its lof - ty halls— a pháis - te bán a stór.— Though—
Au - tumn winds— may droop— and die a bud of spring— are you. Sing—
hush - a - bye, lul, lul, lo, lo, lan, sing hush - a - bye lul, lul, loo.—

Bring no ill wind to hinder us, my helpless babe and me,
Dread spirit of Blackwater banks, Clan Eoin's wild banshee,
And Holy Mary pitying, in heaven for grace doth sue.
Chorus:- (repeat after each verse)

Take time to thrive, my Rose of hope, in the garden of Dromore,
Take heed young Eagle, till your wings are feathered fit to soar.
A little time and then our land is full of things to do.

Bleaching the Linen, Co. Antrim

Nova Scotia

Traditional

Arrangement copyright Waltons Publications Ltd.

Oh fare-well to No-va Sco - tia, the sea-bound coast. Let your moun - tains dark— and drea - ry be. Oh when I'm far a - way o'er the gri - my oc - ean tossed, Will you ev - er hear a sigh— or a wish for me?—

I grieve to leave my native land,
Grieve to leave my comrades all,
And my parents whom I held so dear,
And the bonny bonny lassie that I do adore.
Repeat first verse:–

The drums do beat and the wars do alarm,
And the captain's call we must obey.
So farewell, farewell, to Nova Scotia's charms,
For it's early in the morning I'll be far, far away.
Repeat first verse:–

I have three brothers and they are at rest,
And their arms are folded on their breast.
But a poor simple sailor just like me,
Must be tossed and driven on the dark blue sea.
Repeat first verse:–

An Irish Mountain Cottage

Banna Strand

This song tells of an attempt by the 1916 patriot, Roger Casement, to land rifles at Banna Strand, Co. Kerry.
His attempt failed and he was executed in London. His body was brought back to Ireland in 1965.

Arrangement copyright Waltons Publications Ltd.

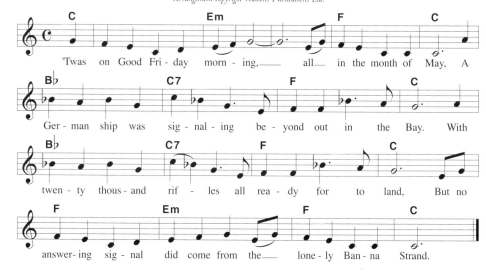

'Twas on Good Fri - day morn - ing,— all— in the month of May, A
Ger - man ship was sig - nal - ing be - yond out in the Bay. With
twen - ty thous - and rif - les all rea - dy for to land, But no
answer- ing sig - nal did come from the— lone - ly Ban - na Strand.

A motorcar was dashing through the early morning gloom,
A sudden crash, and in the stream they went to meet their doom.
Two Irish lads were dying there just like their hopes so grand,
They could not give the signal now from the lonely Banna Strand.

'No signal answers from the shore,' Sir Roger sadly said.
'No comrades here to meet me, alas they must be dead.
But I must do my duty, and at once I mean to land.'
So in a small boat rowed ashore to the lonely Banna Strand.

The R.I.C. were hunting for Sir Roger high and low.
They found him at McKenna's fort, they said, 'You are our foe.'
Said he, 'I'm Roger Casement. I came to my native land.
I mean to free my countrymen on the lonely Banna Strand.'

They took Sir Roger prisoner and sailed for London Town,
And in the Tower they laid him, a traitor to the Crown.
Said he, 'I am no traitor,' but his trial he had to stand,
For bringing German rifles to the lonely Banna Strand.

'Twas in an English prison that they led him to his death.
'I'm dying for my country,' he said with his last breath.
They buried him in British soil, far from his native land,
And the wild waves sang his requiem on the lonely Banna Strand.

Big Strong Man (Sylvest)

This old music hall song has become popular among Irish ballad singers.

Arrangement copyright Waltons Publications Ltd.

Have you heard ab-out the big strong man? He lives in a car-a-van. Have you heard ab-out the Jeff-rey John-ston fight? Oh what a hell of a fight. You can take all the hea-vy-weights you got,—— we got a lad who will beat the whole lot. He used to ring the bells in the bel-fry, now he's gon-na fight Jack Demp-sey.

Chorus

Was me bro-ther Syl-vest, what's he got? A row of for-ty me-dals on his chest, big chest, He killed fif-ty bad men in the West, He knows no rest, think of the man, hell's fire don't push just shove, plen-ty of room for you and me. Got an arm like a leg, and a punch that would sink a batt-le ship, big ship, Takes all the ar-my and the na-vy—— to put the wind up Syl-vest.

He thought he'd take a trip to Italy, he thought that he'd go by sea,
He dived off the harbour in New York, he swam like a great big shark.
He saw the Lusitania in distress, put the Lusitania on his chest,
Drank all the water in the sea, he walked all the way to Italy.
Chorus:—

He thought he'd take a trip to old Japan, they brought out the big brass band,
He played every instrument they'd got, what a lad, he played the whole lot.
The old church bell will ring, the old church choir will sing,
They all turned out to say farewell, to my big brother Sylvest.
Chorus-

An Od Irish Village

I'll Take You Home Again Kathleen

Thomas Paine Westendorf, an American, was said to have written this song for his
wife Jenny. They were both of German origin and longed to return to their homeland.

Arrangement copyright Waltons Publications Ltd.

I know you love me, Kathleen dear, your heart was ever fond and true.
I always feel when you are near, that life holds nothing dear but you.
The smiles that once you gave to me, I scarcely ever see them now,
Though many, many times I see a dark'ning shadow on your brow.
Chorus:-

To that dear home beyond the sea, my Kathleen shall again return,
And when thy old friends welcome thee, thy loving heart will cease to yearn.
Where laughs the little silver stream, beside your mother's humble cot,
And brighter rays of sunshine gleam, there all your grief will be forgot.
Chorus:-

The Enniskillen Dragoon

George Sigerson (1839-1920), born in Holyhill, near Strabane, Co. Tyrone, earned himself the title 'The Grand Old Man of Literature' for his many poems and songs. He was associated with members of the IRB.

Arrangement copyright Waltons Publications Ltd.

Fare thee well En - nis - kil- len, fare thee well for a while, To all your fair wa - ters and ev' - ry green isle. Oh your green Isle will flour- ish, your fair wa- ters will flow, While— I from old Ire - land an ex- ile must go.—

They were all dressed out like gentlemen's sons,
With their bright shining swords and carbine guns,
With their silver mounted pistols, she observed them full soon,
Because that she loved her Enniskillen Dragoon.

The bright sons of Mars, as they stood on the right,
Their armour did shine like the bright stars at night.
Says she, 'Lovely Willie, you've listed too soon,
To serve as a Royal Enniskillen Dragoon.'

'O beautiful Flora, your pardon I crave,
Until now and forever, I will be your slave.
Your parents insult you both morning and noon,
For fear you should wed your Enniskillen Dragoon.'

'O now, dearest Willie, mind what you say,
For children are obliged their parents to obey.
But when you're leaving Ireland, they all change their tune,
Saying, the Lord be with you, Enniskillen Dragoon.'

Farewell Enniskillen, farewell for a while,
And all around the borders of Erin's Isle.
And when the wars are over, you'll return in full bloom,
They'll all welcome home the Enniskillen Dragoon.

Now the war is over, and they have returned at last,
The regiment lies in Dublin, and Willie's got a pass.
Last Sunday they were married, and Willie was the groom,
And now she enjoys her Enniskillen Dragoon.

The Black Velvet Band

A tragic song about Van Dieman's Land, now Tasmania, named after the Dutchman who discovered it. Many people were transported there by the British, often for petty crimes, causing misery for families and loved ones.

Arrangement copyright Waltons Publications Ltd.

'Twas in the town of Tralee, an apprentice to trade I was bound,
With a-plenty of bright amusement to see the days go round.
'Till misfortune and trouble came over me, which caused me to stray from my land,
Far away from my friends and relations, to follow the black velvet band.
Chorus:-

As I went walking down Broadway, not intending to stay very long,
I met with a frolicsome damsel, as she came tripping along.
A watch she pulled out of her pocket and slipped it right into my hand,
On the very first day that I met her, bad luck to that black velvet band.
Chorus:-

Before judge and jury, the both of us had to appear,
And a gentleman swore to the jewellery, the case against us was clear.
Seven long years transportation right down unto Van Diemen's Land,
Far away from my friends and relations, betrayed by the black velvet band.
Chorus:-

Come all you brave young Irish lads, a warning take by me,
Beware the pretty young damsels that go tripping around in Tralee.
They'll treat you to whiskey and porter, until you're unable to stand,
And before you have time for to leave them, you are unto Van Diemen's Land.
Chorus:-

Oft in the Stilly Night

Another beautiful song by Thomas Moore (1779-1852).

Arrangement copyright Waltons Publications Ltd.

When I remember all the friends so linked together,
I've seen around me fall, like leaves in wint'ry weather,
I feel like one who treads alone, some banquet hall deserted,
Whose lights are fled, whose garlands dead, and all but he departed.
Thus in the stilly night ere slumber's chain has bound me,
Sad mem'ry brings the light of other days around me.

The Gay Galtee Mountains

Traditional

Arrangement copyright Waltons Publications Ltd.

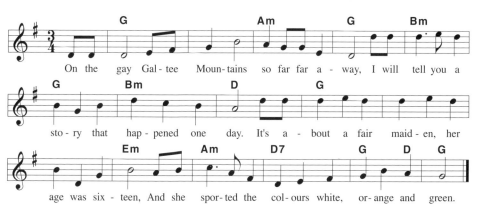

On the gay Gal-tee Moun-tains so far far a-way, I will tell you a sto-ry that hap-pened one day. It's a-bout a fair maid-en, her age was six-teen, And she spor-ted the col-ours white, or-ange and green.

A young British soldier was passing that way,
And he spied the fair maiden with colours so gay.
He rode alongside her, jumped off his machine,
And he tried for to capture the flag of Sinn Féin.

'You'll not get these colours,' the fair maiden said.
'You'll not get these colours until I am dead.
I'll fight by the glenside, it remains to be seen,
And I'll die for my country, white, orange and green.'

'Twas early next morning in Tipperary town,
From the gay Galtee Mountains the young maiden came down.
She was sick in her heart, it was plain to be seen,
For they murdered Tom Ashe for the flag of Sinn Féin.

A Mountain Cottage

The Maid of the Sweet Brown Knowe

'Knowe' is a small hill or knoll.

Arrangement copyright Waltons Publications Ltd.

Come— all ye lads— and lass-ies, and lis-ten to me a while,— And I'll
sing for you a verse or two which will cause you all to smile.— It's
all a-bout a young man, and I'm going to tell you how,— He—
late-ly came— a-court-ing of the Maid of the Sweet Brown Knowe.—

Said he, 'My pretty fair maid, will you come along with me?
We'll both go off together, and married we will be.
We'll join our hands in wedlock bands, I'm speaking to you now,
And I'll do my best endeavour for the Maid of the Sweet Brown Knowe.'

This fair and fickle young thing, she knew not what to say,
Her eyes did shine like silver bright and merrily did play.
She said, 'Young man your love subdue, for I am not ready now,
And I'll spend another season at the foot of the Sweet Brown Knowe.'

Said he, 'My pretty fair maid, how can you answer so?
Look down on yonder valley, where my crops do gently grow.
Look down on yonder valley, where my horses, men and plough
Are at their daily labour for the Maid of the Sweet Brown Knowe.'

'If they're at their daily labour, kind sir, it's not for me,
For I've heard of your behaviour, I have indeed,' said she.
'There is an inn where you call in, I've heard the people say,
Where you rap and call and pay for all, and go home at the break of day.'

'If I rap and call and pay for all, the money is all my own,
And I'll never spend your fortune, for I hear you have got none.
You thought you had my poor heart broke in talking with me now,
But I'll leave you where I found you, at the foot of the Sweet Brown Knowe.'

The Banks of Claudy

Traditional

Arrangement copyright Waltons Publications Ltd.

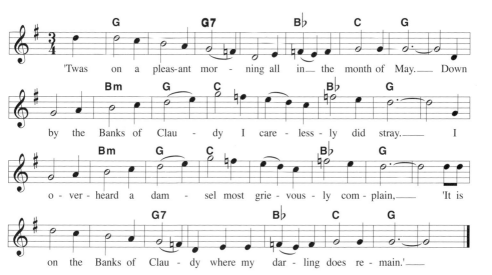

'Twas on a pleas-ant mor - ning all in— the month of May.— Down
by the Banks of Clau - dy I care - less - ly did stray.— I
o - ver - heard a dam - sel most grie - vous - ly com - plain,— 'It is
on the Banks of Clau - dy where my dar - ling does re - main.'—

I boldly stepped up to her, I took her by surprise,
I own she did not know me, I being dressed in disguise.
'Where are you going my fair one, my joy and heart's delight,
Where are you going to wander, this dark and stormy night?'

'It's on the way to Claudy's banks if you will please to show,
Take pity on a stranger, for there I want to go.
It's seven long years or better since Johnny has left this shore,
He's crossing the wide ocean, where the foaming billows roar.'

'He's crossing the wide ocean for honour and for fame,
His ship's been wrecked, so I've been told, down on the Spanish Main.'
'It's on the banks of Claudy, fair maid, whereon you stand,
Now don't you believe young Johnny, for he's a false young man.'

Now when she heard this dreadful news, she fell into despair,
For the wringing of her tender hands and the tearing of her hair.
'If Johnny he be drowned, no man alive I'll take.
Through lonesome shades and valleys, I'll wander for his sake.'

Now when he saw her loyalty, no longer could he stand,
He fell into her arms, saying, 'Betsy, I'm the man.'
Saying, 'Betsy, I'm the young man that caused you all your pain,
And since we've met on Claudy's banks, we'll never part again.'

The Rocks of Bawn

Up until the 1950s, the hiring fair was the most popular way to acquire staff (spalpeens)
to work and live on the farm, usually for a six-month period.

Arrangement copyright Waltons Publications Ltd.

Come — all ye loy - al— he - roes and list - en— un - to
me.— Don't hire with an - y— far - mer till you know what your
work— will— be.— You will rise up ear - ly in the morn -
ing from the clear day - light till— the dawn,— and you nev - er
will be— ab - le for to plough the— Rocks of Bawn.—

My shoes they are worn and my stockings they are thin,
My heart is always trembling now, for fear they might give in.
My heart is always trembling now, from the clear daylight till the dawn,
And I never will be able for to plough the Rocks of Bawn.

Rise up, gallant Sweeney, and get your horses hay,
And give them a good feed of oats before they start away.
Don't feed them on soft turnip sprigs that grow on your green lawn,
Or they never will be able for to plough the Rocks of Bawn.

My curse upon you, Sweeney boy, you have me nearly robbed,
You're sitting by the fireside now, your feet upon the hob.
You're sitting by the fireside now, from the clear daylight till the dawn,
And you never will be able for to plough the Rocks of Bawn.

I wish the Sergeant-Major would send for me in time,
And place me in some regiment all in my youth and prime.
I'd fight for Ireland's glory now, from the clear daylight till the dawn,
Before I would return again to plough the Rocks of Bawn.